Coimbra

Everest Editora would like to thank you for purchasing this book. It has been
created by an extensive and complete publishing team made up of photographers,
illustrators and authors specialised in the field of tourism, together with our modern
cartography department. Everest guarantees that the contents of this work were completely
up to date at the time of going to press, and we would like to invite you to send us any
information that helps us to improve our publications, so that we may always offer
QUALITY TOURISM.

QUALITY
TOURISM
WITH
EVEREST

Please send your comments to:
Everest Editora Lda.
Apartado 168 – 2635 Rio de Mouro
everesteditora@mail.telepac.pt

Text and photographs: Pedro Pinto

Editorial Board: Raquel López Varela

Editorial coordenation: Eva María Fernández, Carla Rodrigues Pires

Diagram: José Manuel Núñez

Cover concept: Alfredo Anievas

Digital treatment of images: David Aller

Cartography: © EVEREST

Translation: Marisa Roberto

© EVEREST EDITORA, Lda.

Parque Industrial Meramar II, amz. 1 e 2
2635-047 Rio de Mouro PORTUGAL
ISBN: 972-750-775-1
Legal deposit: 175873/02
Printing date: February 2002
Printed in Spain

Editorial Evergráficas, S. L.
Carretera León-La Coruña, km 5
LEÓN (Spain)

The patio of the University (16th-18th century).

A VIEW OVER THE CITY

The best place to obtain an overall view of Coimbra might still be the old belvedere situated at the bottom end of the street which, for centuries, served as the link between the city and the southern-centre part of the country, with Lisbon, its capital, it is a road stretch that is almost totally reduced to establishing contact with one of the periphereal areas of the city. Suspended over the flattened valley through which runs the Mondego River, a denomination which is still maintained to designate the depths engraved by the waters, it seems to want to recollect a configuration from another era, characterized then by very sloping walls. It is the very aptly named Valley of Hell *(Vale do Inferno)*, of which the belvedere was to assume the name.

And then we came across the old Coimbra, tucked away in a steep hill. Over the left, dominating the old row of houses of the city, above all else, rises the top of the 7th-century University tower. More visibly, and surrounding this tower, are the walls of the old royal "Alcáçova" and the edifice of the Joanina Library, endowed with enormous windows. Immediately on the right, one comes across the wide courtyard of the University and, next, the whole block of more modern University buildings, the construction of which, programmed in the Forties, begins the following decade and continues into the Sixties and further, into the first half of the Seventies. On another plain, the shadow of the row of houses, which is stretched to the north and to the source of the old hill, is clearly delienated.

At the bottom, in the valley flattened by the sediments gradually brought on by the waters of the Mondego on winterish days, runs the river, now forming here as if a lake, a mirror of water, its course having since become regular by a dam bridge, situated at the downstream side of the road bridge. On this side of the river, stretched out, are the cultivated fields, in which the orange-blossom trees of Coimbra, that were once famous, sprout. More famous still, however, is the Homestead of Tears *(Quinta das Lágrimas)*, implanted in these riverside fields, a place renowned that legend associated to the hidden loves of Inês de Castro and Prince Pedro, who would come to reign under the title of King Pedro I.

Still on the left bank, immediately by the exit of the road bridge, whoever comes from Coimbra via the old road, enters the Santa Clara suburb, which took on the name of the most sought-after of the convents set out on the southern bank of the Mondego River: the Convent of Santa Clara. Actually, the suburb assumed the name of two successive convents dedicated to Santa Clara, the old and the new. *Santa Clara-a-Velha* (Old Santa Clara), the *coenobium* innundated by the waters of the river and invaded by the alluvial soil, and *Santa Clara-a-Nova* (New Santa Clara), the elongated and imposing edifice situated at the tip of the Hill of Hope *(Monte de Esperança)* and to where the Clarist nuns moved in the second half of the 6th-century, permanently abandonning the primitive installations they once used to occupy.

The University and the row of houses of Alta.

◀ *The courtyard of the University. The Manueline portal of the St. Michael Chapel (Capela de S. Miguel), and the seventh-century Tower (Torre) and gallery (Via Latina).*

ANOTHER VIEW

To commence this visit to Coimbra I suggest to the reader that, from here, from the belvedere of the Valley of Hell *(Vale do Inferno)* he descend, now, down to the road bridge, leaving for much later the corresponding way to the Santa Clara suburb. Let us now cross the Mondego river, to its right bank. Here, one faces the compact row of houses of the city, which haughtily rises above the hillock in which its primitive inhabitants first settled, surely well before the Roman militaries, the public servants, and the traders were to occupy the locale where the city they named *Aeminium* (or *Emínio,* to use a more Portuguese version) was erected.

In front of us, the south and the south-setting sunny hillside descends. The city profile is now much more limited than when we viewed it from the top of the Valley of Hell *(Vale do Inferno).* Bathed by the soft late afternoon light of the sun, the row of houses are arranged stagger-like, in amphitheatre-form. The tower of the University, with its clock and its enclosed narrow balcony, above which, on festive days, floats the national flag, rises above the roof of the old fortress. From this vantage point, one can see the back of the Manueline chapel, the three enormous windows of the posterior facade of the Joanine Library *(Biblioteca Joanina),* whilst one or another residential edifice, quite ordinary, seem also to want to stand out in this set scenario of the old acropolis.

Once down here, closing on the level of the river, and quite transformed, one discerns the existence of one of the towers of the old medieval enclosure wall, a fragment of wall in well-prepared stone. Bordering the course of the river waters, immediately to the upstream side of the bridge, is a long row of rounded treetops marking out the limit of the City Park *(Parque da Cidade).*

The elegant cement bridge that crosses the Mondego – and which is designated the Santa Clara bridge *(Ponte de Santa Clara)* – encloses the subsisting traces of yet another older bridge, built in the sixteenth-century, buried in the sands, of which remain the still visible stones from the beginning of the arches that supported the demolished tray, when the lowering in the level of the waters allows us to observe them. In front of us, triangular, and seemingly dispersing into the edges of a funnel, opens up the *Largo da Portagem* – to recollect the (toll) levy that was charged to all those who crossed the bridge, – a funnel, the mouth of which runs into Ferreira Borges Street *(Rua Ferreira Borges).* But, before going on, we would like to remind our reader of how the torrent of the river, thorugh a range of milennia and of centuries, came to drag the debris, the soils, the eroded materials of the mountainous slopes through which the Mondego runs. It was, thus, that the level of its bed was raised and how, bit by bit, the waters increasingly came to flood its banks, spreading soil and sand, burying roads, squares and edifices. Such was the case, as we saw, of the medieval Santa Clara Convent *(Convento de Santa Clara),* on the left bank. Likewise, so it happened to the riverside urban zone, stretched along the right bank of the river. Thus, too, with this *Largo da Portagem,* today a few metres higher in relation to its Middle Ages bed level, for example.

An open view over the city.

THE CITY CENTRE (BAIXA)

The square in which we find ourselves now is a slightly landscaped small square, in the middle of which rises the statue of a politician from the nineteenth-century who became famous for having passed, in 1834, around the time of the instauration of the liberal order, the Act that dissemated the religious orders in Portugal. He was called Joaquim António de Aguiar, but here, forevermore, he was attributed the nickname for which he still known today – the *Mata-Frades* or the Friar-Killer.

The group of edifices that marks the space of the *Portagem* hardly has a notable design, an exception being the one that was expressly constructed, in 1912, in the first years of the nineteenth-century, as the headquarters of the Bank of Portugal. This one does, indeed, reveal a highly defined architectonic character and with which, in chronological terms and in terms of project authorship, a neighbour edifice, seen here in a corner perspective – a corner that is narrow and rounded, crowned by a dome – the Astória Hotel, immediately next door, is closely related. Both edifices were created by the same man, the architect Arnaldo Adães Bermudes.

Barred to the traffic, the square has undoubtedly become one of the most pleasant "in" places to be in the whole city. The esplanades of the cafés strewn over the little square offer, right away, to the visitor the image of a "quiet Coimbra", an image which is not unfounded, since the city nevertheless preserves – and, not withstanding the urban expansion that it has come to know in more recent decades – the pleasant atmosphere of a provincial city.

The square opens up into an extensive pedestrian artery which, structured in a northerly direction, is prolonged right up to the crossroads situated close to the Municipal Council *(Câmara Municipal)* edifice, an intersection of roads, namely of the Direita, the Olímpio Nicolau Fernandes and the Sofia Roads. The long artery includes the Ferreira Borges and the Visconde de Luz Roads, which were previously, and respectively, designated the *Calçada* and the Coruche Road. The designation of the first stretch of the way – *Calçada* – seems to want to recollect the one Roman road that, coming from *Olisipo* (the current Lisbon), passed through *Sellium* (known today as Tomar) and through Conímbriga, served *Aeminium* (Coimbra) and headed north, having as its principal destiny, *Braccara Augusta* (Braga), the capital of Calécia.

The first half of this route, the Ferreira Borges Road, seems to maintain its outlined ancient traces, of at least the last three, or even, four centuries. The Visconde da Luz Road, on the other hand, suffered an increase in its width, with particular incidence in the second half of the nineteenth-century. Both are roads of intense commercial activity, of an often luxury-type of commerce, traditionally aimed at the satisfaction of the needs of a clientele that is endowed with a strong purchasing power, as opposed to the one that is conducted in the little roads that make up the old City Centre *(Baixa Velha)*. Adjacent to this artery of strong mercantile vocation, the old City Centre *(Baixa Velha)* has its noble space configured as it is, in the Square of Commerce *(Praça do Comércio)* – also known as the Old Square *(Praça Velha)*, and in it, a certain type of business is conducted, in which the products and the prices, that are more suited to the tastes and the possibilities of the popular classes, are dominant.

◄ *The Toll-gate Square (Praça da Portagem). The float of the Burning of the Ribbons (Queima das Fitas).*

Toll-gate Square (Praça da Portagem). The statue of Mata-Frades (1911). ►

Toll-gate Square (Praça da Portagem). The Bank of Portugal and Astória Hotel buildings.

The Road of Sofia (Rua da Sofia). ▶

At the entrance to Ferreira Borges Road.

The Ferreira Borges Road. An old store.

On the day of Queima das Fitas.

And by referring to popular classes, we understand by that, not only the people of Coimbra of more modest means but also the peasants, originally from the surrounding little villages, which, amble, ant-like, in direction of the city, namely when they come to sell their agricultural products and, simultaneously, to stock up on goods (and even to resort to a certain type of more specialized service...) which are not so readily available in their local village shops.

The Old Square (Praça do Comércio).

The Old City Centre *(Baixa Velha)* used to function traditionally – and in some ways still does – as a platform of reunion between the small urban people (small traders, artisans,...) and the rural world that surrounds the city. The whole area, thus, would be populated by a small crowd which would fill up the narrow roads of the city centre with movement. This explanation also helps us to understand the proliferation, in this same city centre, of taverns and eating houses which, in the modesty of their installations, are still able to match, in terms of culinary confection, many of the more pretentious existing restaurants in Coimbra.

But today, it is certain that the ambience is changing. On a par with the alterations in economic and cultural conditions, in the transformation of mentalities, the implementation of urban shopping centres in the urban periphery and the installation of the greater commercial areas have brought, with them, a modification in the consumer habits which no longer similarly characterize the abovementioned picture. Nevertheless, the commercial activity in this nobler artery, made up of the Ferreira Borges and Visconde da Luz Roads, remains very much alive. Expensive clothes-shops, pharmacies, jewellers, bookshops, coffe-shops, bakeries, etc., pratically occupy all the lower floors of the existing buildings in this axis, reserved for some years for the pedestrian traffic.

Business in the city centre streets.

The eating house «O Mija Gato». ▶

Almedina Arch (Arco da Almedina) (9th-15th century)

Let us leave, for now, the Old City Centre *(Baixa Velha)* which stretches towards the west of the road axis, on a lower level. Proceeding straight on down Ferreira Borges Road, we eventually came across an arch of medieval origin, but since altered in the sixteenth-century, the Arch of Barbacã *(Arco da Barbacã)*, a term which identifies that wall of reduced thickness and of reduced height that served as a rampart fence to the more robust walls of the larger fence, that protected the city. Next, we find the opening which, actually, allows for access into the inter-mural zone, just a little above it. It is the opening in the extremely strong enclosure wall, designated as the Arch of Almedina *(Arco da Almedina)*, that permitted entrance directly into the residential heart of the borough, the almedina.

◀ *Barbacã Arch (Arco da Barbacã)(a fifth-century reconstruction).*

◄ *The University courtyard. The statue of King João 111 (1948).*

The Church of Saint Cross (Igreja de Santa Cruz)(facade from the 16th-century).

The Palace of Sobre Ripas (Palácio de Sobre Ripas). A Manueline portal

The old cathedral (Sé Velha), a romantic church.

THE ALMEDINA

Almedina – a word, of Arabic origin, which designated one of the parts which made up the whole fortified urban area. The other part, the palatine zone, suspended on the top of the hill, lodged the political and military power – the royal palace or that of the Governor, the High Commissioners, and the permanent military corps. It was the castle – a word of similar Arab origin – where, in the concrete case of Coimbra, the University was finally established, in the sixteenth-century, in 1537, in the quarters that had been granted by King D. João III.

And it is precisely in the direction of the University that we will go on walking. In front of us, a well-traced, straight road rips open, the old *Rua das Fangas*, or should we say, the road, known today as the Fernandes Tomás Road, in which the houses that kept the bread, the grain were situated. It is a slightly sloping road, which gently ascends. It runs parallel to the south stretch of the Ferreira Borges Road (the one known as *Calçada*). Hidden among the row of houses that is situated in the space between both, runs, in turn, a stretch of road that is probably a remnant of the old medieval enclosure wall.

The extension of this old *Rua das Fangas* would take us up to a new fortified zone, in a place where there are two paths denominated *"couraça"* – the Estrela one, which descends in the direction of the Santa Clara Bridge *(Ponte de Santa Clara)* and the Toll-gate Square *(Praça da Portagem)*, and the Lisbon one, which ends up converging on the previous one, beginning at the high part of the hill in which the

University City is installed. In this place, one of the doors of the medieval enclosure wall, the *Porta de Belcouce*, was to be found, having been demolished in the nineteenth-century. The cuirass was an extension of the fortified wall, attached to the principal enclosure wall, which allowed access to the river, an access that was direct and safe. A door flanked by two towers – the cuirass door – opened up directly onto the waters of the Mondego.

Once again at the entrance of the almedina, and after having cleared its high arch, we realize how accentuated the slope of the hill, where the row of Coimbran houses is, actually is. In front of us rises a steep ascent that is so sloped that the city administrators thought it wise to soften its course, dividing it into steps and landings that were to make the traffic less painful on the citizens. These are the Coast-breaking Steps *(Escadas do Quebra Costas)*, by means of which the slope formed by this coast or slope was "broken", or softened.

The ascent, short, but, nevertheless, still tiring, leads us to discover one of the most important historical and arquitectonic monuments of Coimbra. Upon reaching the last landing, the austere facade of the Old Cathedral *(Sé Velha)*, the old city cathedral rises before us, at an even higher level and served with a stairway. It is a compact facade, formed by three vertical panels of limestone stone wall, with tower-shaped corners. The stone reveals a darkened tone, which gains golden reflexes when the sunset light falls on it.

Romantic chapiters from the old cathedral (Sé Velha).

In the previous double-page, flowering "jacarandás".

A Revivalist house, inspired by the old cathedral (Sé Velha). ▶

The old cathedral (Sé Velha). A romantic chapiter from its portal.

THE OLD CATHEDRAL *(SÉ VELHA)*

The edifice has the robust appearance of a fortress, which is accentuated by the lack of openings and, above all, by the curtain of battlements that crown its cyma. On the central panel, clearly more salient than the lateral ones, two ample openings tear open. One is the entrance portal to the temple which, bordered by pillars and covered by arches, almost creates the space of a churchyard. Above it, is a torn open enormous window, which, in some way, serves as its replica, similarly endowed with lateral pillars and archivolts. The three vertical panels of the facade define the three longitudinal naves into which the temple is divided, so that the centre panel corresponds to the central nave of the church. The apse and the two lateral apsidioles are situated at both extremes of the nave.

The old cathedral (Sé Velha). The cloister.

◀ *The University. Pólo II (Boavista). Nineties decade.*

The temple, planned by an architect of French origin, Master Roberto, was erected, globally, between 1162 and 1184 and constitutes one of the most pure examples of the Romantic style existing in the whole Portuguese territory. Acting as church-cathedral since its origin, it will cease to perform this function when, in the Seventies decade of the eighteenth-century, the cathedral-like title begins to be branched out by the old church belonging to the College of Jesus *(Colégio de Jesus)*, which takes on the designation of New Cathedral *(Sé Nova)*.

Built in the second half of the twelfth-century, the Old Cathedral *(Sé Velha)* will, through the ages, come to know modifications, extensions, innovations. Thus, the cloister which is adjacent to it dates from the first years of the following century, from the reign of King D. Afonso II, and constitutes one of the oldest Gothich constructions undertaken in Portugal, put into practice immediately after the edification of the first Portuguese monument that followed the norms of this new style, the church of the Monastery of Alcobaça *(Mosteiro de Alcaboça)*.

At the end of the fifteenth-century and in the first decades of the following century, the Old Cathedral *(Sé Velha)* will again be subject to transformations, like the ones which altered its northern facade, with the inclusion of two ostentatious doors, in Renaissance-style, worked in soft limestone, a material that has resisted the passing of time with great difficulty. The richer and more ornate one is the *Porta Especiosa,* due to João de Ruão, a French sculptor who settled in Coimbra. Further up we find the Santa Clara Door or *Porta de Santa Clara*, elaborated in a more simple design.

Inside the temple, among many works of great quality, two altarpieces deserve special distinction. One, of painted wood carving, occupies the whole background of the altar-mor and is the work of the Flemish artists Olivier de Gand and Jean d'Ypres, dating from the turn of the fifteenth-century to the next century. The other, decorates the lateral chapel of the Holy Sacrament. It is sculpted in stone of ança and is the artistic product of the abovementioned French sculptor, João de Ruão.

THE UNIVERSITY CITY

Proceeding down the road that skirts the lateral facade of the Old Cathedral *(Sé Velha)*, we run into the full centre of the University City, at the *Largo da Porta Férrea*, circumscribed by two edifices dating from the years 50-60, namely the Faculty of Arts and the Library of the University, and, on the west, by the access gate to the University Patio, the so-called *Porta Férrea*. These, just like the ones that lodge the Faculties of Medicine, of Sciences and of Mathematics, are the result of the great campaign of public works programmed in the years 40, to which we have made reference above, and which was translated into the demolition of a very significant part of the Coimbran *Velha Alta*.

But the heart of the traditional University City resides in the area that is reached when the arch of the six-century *Porta Férrea* is crossed. We are in the Patio of the University. Or, rather, if we prefer, we are in the patio of the old Fortress *(Alcáçova)* granted by King D. João III to the Portuguese University. To our right, runs the seventh-century pillared gallery, the famous *Via Latina,* in the middle of which rises an arched body topped by a pediment. On the extreme end of this gallery emerges the undoubtedly still more famous Tower, built in 1728-33, and the iconographic symbol not only of the University but also of the actual city of Coimbra.

The Square of the Porta Férrea (Praça da Porta Férrea).
On the right, is the edifice of the Faculty of Arts
(1951).

The statue of King Dinis (1943).

◄ *The Square of the Porta Férrea (Praça da Porta Férrea). Monumental statuary – Medicine (1955).*

The patio of the University on the day of the Burning of the Ribbons (Queima das Fitas).

The Joanine portal of the Library (18th-century). ▶

From this same angle open up the *Gerais,* installations that serve the Faculty of Law. Proceeding down this aisle, we come to find two of the most important edifices of the University set: the St Michael Chapel *(Capela de S. Miguel)* with its Manueline portal, that was the old chapel of the *Paço Real,* and the luxurious Library. Built in the time of King D. João V, a work of great ostentation, well in accordance with the era and with the pompous taste of the monarch. The south side of the patio – in which the statue of King D. João III figures- is today free and opens up as a balcony onto the vast horizon, in which the silver lining of the Mondego River is etched. The third wing of the patio is occupied by the block of the now extinct College of St. Peter *(Colégio de S. Pedro).* From among the old edifices that were part of the University set and which resisted the demolitions that took place since the mid -nineteenth-century, two old Colleges, the St. Jeronimo and that of Arts *(S. Jerónimo e das Artes),* both built in the sixteenth-century, should be highlighted. These Colleges lodged the Hospitals of the University for a long time, until the recent implantation of the new Hospital building. Already seventh-century creations, taking us back to the Pombaline era, the two edifices destined for the teachings of Science, the Museum of Natural History *(Museu de História Natural* – which, nevertheless, preserves sixteenth-century elements) and the Chemical Laboratory *(Laboratório Químico),* were both designed according to the NeoClassic style.

The Museum of Natural History (second half of the 18th-century).

The new cathedral (Sé Nova) and the Museum of Natural History (18th-century).

◀ The 5th-century St. Michael Chapel (Capela de S. Miguel).

The Machado de Castro Museum (Museu Machado de Castro). The Gallery.

◀ *On the previous double page, the new cathedral (Sé Nova), the Chapel-mor.*

Connected to the University by its origin, the current New Cathedral *(Sé Nova)* was first constructed as the church annexing the College of Jesus *(Colégio de Jesus)*, an imposing pair built by the priests of the *Companhia*. Once the Jesuits were expelled from the country, in 1759, during the government of the Marquess of Pombal, the church began to perform the functions of a Coimbran cathedral, depriving the old romantic church of this dignity. The New Cathedral *(Sé Nova)* began to be constructed already at the end of the sixteenth-century, but its construction was prolonged throughout the following century. Amply decorated and richly ornamented, the temple is one of the most imposing of the whole city. Inside the University area of the Alta we will also have to highlight the enormous mole constituted by the old St. Augustine College *(Colégio de Santo Agostinho or da Sapiência)*, belonging to the Coimbran Saint Cross friars, with its edification having equally been started in the last years of the sixteenth-century. Still within the Coimbran *Alta,* near the New Cathedral *(Sé Nova)* and the University buildings, emerges the old Bishop's Palace *(Paço Episcopal)*, which today includes the Machado de Castro National Museum *(Museu Nacional Machado de Castro)*. Destined to be the residence of the main figure of the Diocese, the Bishops of Coimbra have boarded here since the medieval era.

*The romantic St. Salvador
Church (Igreja de S. Salvador).*

Largely remodelled in the sixteenth-century and, just as other monuments in the city, in the turn from the fifth-century to the sixth-century, worth highlighting in the building is the open gallery over the city and over the river, a work of extreme elegance and lightness. Transformed into a museum after the implantation of the Republican regime, in 1910, its lot in medieval and Renaissance sculpture is particularly notable. Extremely curious and important is the fact that all the construction rests on a complex gallery erected in the Roman era – the cryptoportico – destined to level an area capable of being used as a principal public square – the *forum* – of the city of *Aeminium*.

Next to the museum edifice, and even integrated into it, we find a church, the Church of St. John of Almedina *(Igreja de s. João de Almedina)*, almost totally reconstructed and where architectonic elements, recuperated in edifices victimised by renovations and tree felling, converge. From among the historical edifications existing in the *Velha Alta*, let us mention also, in this zone, the romantic church of St. Salvador *(Igreja de S. Salvador)*. Or, already in the proximity of the *Colégio da Sapiência*, the Tower of Anto *(Torre de Anto)*, one of the towers of the medieval fence tha t was adapted into a residence, and where the poet António Nobre lived. Immediately there, too, is the Palace of the Sub-Ripas *(Palácio de Sub-Ripas)*, a mansion dating from the mid- sixteenth-century, both in close proximity to the College of St. Augustine *(Colégio de Santo Agostinho)*.

The Inkas Republic. ▶

Student satire: "Dux Veteranasnum".

A Republican warning...

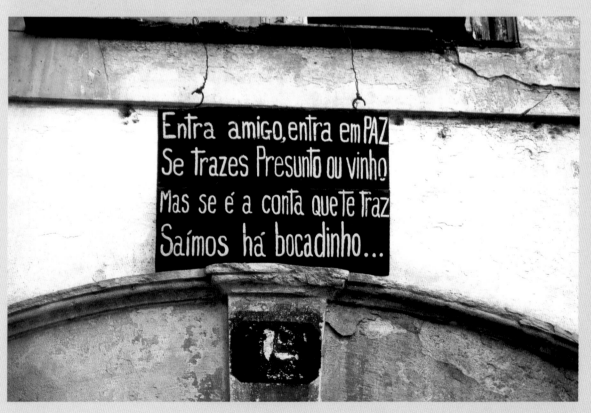

Dominated by the University city, the old Alta *(Velha Alta)* still shelters a numerous student population and, along the streets, it is not difficult to came across some of the traditional student residences, self-managed, by one or the other Republic, which are identified by an irreverent exterior decoration and by their own designations, revealed in an identifying plaque: the Baco Republic, the Kágados Republic, the Inkas Republic...

John Paul II in the Arches of the Garden (Arcos do Jardim).

THE LOW CITY *(CIDADE BAIXA)* ONCE AGAIN

From the D. Dinis Square *(Largo de D. Dinis)*, one can follow the arches of the aqueduct, the construction of which was commanded, in the sixteenth-century, during the reign of D. Sebastião, the so-called Arches of the Garden *(Arcos do Jardim)*, close to which a statue of the Pope John Paul II was erected. Yet another old University College, the S. Bento College, is adjacent to one of the most interesting botannical gardens of the whole country. This one, Coimbra's own, owes its existence to the initiative of the Marquess of Pombal. Further on from the garden, is the *Seminário Maior*, constructed around the mid-seventh-century. Now, and fully integrated into a residential area, in a landscaped place with a belvedere facing the nascent, one finds one of the most recollected places of Coimbran student romanticism, the *Penedo da Saudade*, with its marble plaques, commemorative of students' reunions or engraved with poems that are greatly evocative of academic life.

The Botanical Garden (18th-century).

Penedo da Saudade.

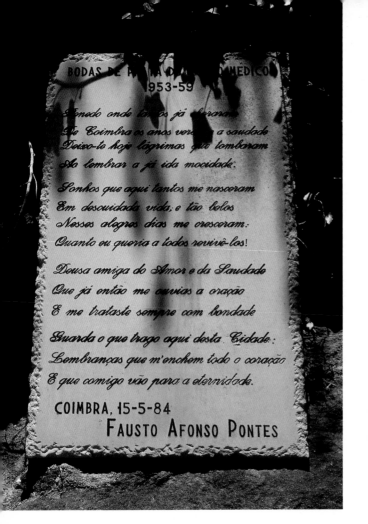

Penedo da Saudade – nostalgic feelings of Coimbra.   *Penedo da Saudade. A bust of António Nobre, the poet.*

Still from the *Largo de D. Dinis*, the Monumental Stairway *(Escadas Monumentais)*, an imponent stairway, descends and leads to the headquarters of the Students Academic Association of Coimbra (1957), to the Square of the Republic *(Praça da República)*, with its esplanades, one of the socialising centres of the student population. Immediately next to the vast square, opens up, by means of an ostentatious portico, one of the most beautiful gardens of the city of Coimbra, normally denominated the Mermaid's Garden *(Jardim da Sereia)*. It is a forested and landscaped place that used to be part of the hedge of the Agostinho de Santa Cruz Monastery *(Mosteiro Agostinho de Santa Cruz)*, a hedge that was shredded after the destruction of the conventual house.

From the Square of the Republic *(Praça da República)*, descending Sá da Bandeira Avenue *(Avenida Sá da Bandeira)*, we proceed through lands that were once the property of that same monastery. Further down from the Municipal Market *(Mercado Municipal)* and immediately next to the old Central Post Office *(Estação Central de Correios)*, is the miniscule Manga Garden *(Jardim da Manga)*, ultimately, merely an erudite fifth-century construct, inspired by the Fountain of Life *(Fonte da Vida)*, that occupied the centre of one of the conventual cloisters. Next, we have, on the other side of the road, what is left of the infirmary and of the barn belonging to the Coimbran Saint Cross friars. Bypassing this last one, a short road opens up that leads us to the Patio of Inquisition *(Pátio da Inquisição)*, an institution that, in 1566, was to occupy the edifice of the College of Arts *(Colégio das Artes)* which, in turn, had succeeded the Colleges of All Saints and of St. Michael *(Colégios de Todos os Santos and de S.Miguel)*. We have now returned to the previously mentioned intersection of the Olímpio Nicolau Fernandes Road, Sofia Road and Direita Road, the latter running into the 8th of May Square *(Largo 8 de Maio)*, the old *Largo de Sansão*. This last one, opening onto the Visconde da Luz Road, acts above all as an access platform to the labyrinth of roads that form the bustling Old City Centre *(Baixa Velha)* which we have also previously referred.

The Students Academic
Association of Coimbra (1957).
The Gil Vicente Theatre.

The Students Academic
Association (1957).
The interior garden.

The Students Academic
Association (1957). Tiled-panel
by João Abel Manta.

The Mermaid's Garden
(Jardim da Sereia).

The "mermaid-man" who gave the garden its name...

◄ The Mermaid's Garden (Jardim da Sereia). Open portico over the Square of the Republic (Praça da República).

◀ *The Sá da Bandeira Avenue Garden (Jardim da Avenida Sá da Bandeira).*

The New Fountain (Fonte Nova).

The "art deco" – inspired Post Office.

The Manga Garden (Jardim da Manga) (16th-century). ▶

The Municipal market.

Trade in the streets of the City centre.

◀ *The romanic Santiago Church (Igreja de Santiago).*

Via them, we also gain access to the Old Square *(Praça Velha)*, a vast space widened in a longitudinal sense, evoking, be it with some justification or not, the form of a Roman "circus". In any event a public square, an area not only commercial but also a place of leisure and of festivity. A space that is ennobled by the existence, in its extreme ends, of two old churches, both previously mentioned, at least, in the twelfth.century, the St Tiago Church *(Igreja de S. Tiago)*, which maintains its Romanic-style characteristics, and the Church of St. Bartholomew *(Igreja de S. Bartolomeu)*, the oldest, which was completely transformed in the eighteenth-century.

But in the 8th of May Square *(Praça 8 de Maio)*, the distinction goes to one of the most noble edifices of the city of Coimbra – on a par with the Old Cathedral *(Sé Velha)* and with the set of University buildings, – the Santa Cruz Monastery *(Mosteiro de Santa Cruz)*, of the Augustine monks. Begun to be built in 1131 – and thus dated prior to the edifice of the Cathedral *(Sé)*, – it suffered great transformations since the beginning of the sixteenth-century, since the Manueline era. Its facade was altered at this time, by a richly sculptured portal, due to artists like a Nicolay Chanterene, a João de Ruão...

The interior of the church was equally completely redone. In the chapel-mor, are featured the fifth-century tombs of the Kings Afonso Henriques and of his son Snacho I, both framed by two finely worked arches. Precious is the Renaissance pulpit of the church. Both the Cloister of Silence *(Claustro de Silêncio)*, fifth-century too, and the vestry, dating from the beginning of the seventeenth-century, are works of great architectonic interest.

On the previous page, the conventual Church of Santa Cruz (Igreja de Santa Cruz): the 5th-century facade; images of the facade; the royal tomb, in the Chapel-mor (16th-century); the pulpit (16th-century).

The Santa Cruz Convent (Convento de Santa Cruz). The mess-hall (16th-century). ▶

The conventual Santa Cruz Church (Igreja de Santa Cruz). The treasure.

The road of Sofia *(Rua de Sofia)* constitutes one of the most notable urbanistic undertakings in the whole of Coimbra city. Beginning in its existence as an area of expansion of the Monastery of Santa Cruz *(Mosteiro de Santa Cruz)*, the road of Sofia was to be ripped, in all its extension, from 1537, precisely at the time when the Portuguese University was to be installed in Coimbra. It was there that the University colleges, supporting the institution established in Alta, were to be built.

If some of the College edifices were demolished or greatly altered, others, be it the temples to which they were annexed, or be it the actual edifices in which the scholars were boarding, still remain standing. Thus, we have the Carmo Gollege, the Graça College, the S. Pedro

◀ *The Santa Cruz Convent (Convento de Santa Cruz). The cloister (16th-century*

The Church of the Graça College (Igreja do Colégio de Graça) (16th-century).

College, the S. Tomás College (which is today known as the Palace of Justice – or *Palácio de Justiça)...* With the Road of Sofia dying out in the Church of Santa Justa *(Igreja de Santa Justa)*, this one much later, since its edification was begun in the first years of the eighteenth-century. Meanwhile, it might not be uninteresting to prolong this course, beginning from the Road of Sofia, following onto the Arnado area and then, going along the Fernão Magalhães Avenue until the *Largo da Portagem* is reached. Between the less interesting row of houses and the rundown areas, one is able to discover some of the most significant Modernist edifices of the city, dating from the Thirties and the Forties, an epoch which seems to have lacked the strength to assert itself over the Revivalist taste of the eighth-century, which was very deep-rooted in the Coimbran architecture of the first ten years of the twentieth-century.

The Church of the Carmo College (Igreja do Colégio do Carmo) (16th-17th-century).

The Palace of Justice (Palácio da Justiça) (the old St. Thomas College – Colégio de S. Tomás).

Auto-Industrial. Modernism of the Thirties, in an ample scale. ▶

The Church of Saint Just (Igreja de Santa Justa) (beginning of the 18th-century).

*The Post Office
(in modern days...)*

A private building. Modernism endures.

The Mondego Hotel. A somber Modernism.

*The Astória Hotel. A "belle
époque" luxury.*

*The old Tivoli Cinema.
The Fifties and the Sixties.*

The Saint Francisco Monastery (Mosteiro de S. Francisco) (17th-century).

PERIPHEREAL AREAS

Coimbra was famous for its periphereal areas in relation to the heart of the city – the high *(Alta)* and the low *(Baixa)* -, many of which, in other times, were authentic rural territories. The neighbourhood of Santa Clara was right there, on the other side of the Mondego. In it, were erected convents – the Santana, the S. Francisco and the Santa Clara convents – which the river destroyed over time. Of the three, only the ruined medieval church of this last one remains standing. For the Franciscans, a new edifice was built in a close place, already at the beginning of the seventeenth-century, a place which is now abandoned.

The Santa Clara Monastery (Mosteiro de Santa Clara) (17th-century).

Portugal dos Pequenitos (1937-44) – a miniature of the University.

Portugal dos Pequenitos (1937-44) – giants for an hour.

◀ *The statue of Isabel de Aragão, the Holy Queen.*

*Homestead of Tears
(Quinta das Lágrimas).
Make-believe ruins
(19th-century).*

*The University. Pólo II
(the Nineties).*

*The Celas Monastery
(Mosteiro de Celas).
The frontispiece (16th-17th-century).*

The new convent of the Clarists was constructed around the middle of the same century and is still visible, imposing in stature, beyond that of Saint Francisco, at the top of the Hill of Hope *(Monte de Esperança)*. Furthermore, what could be contradictorily called a kind of monumental Portugal in miniature, the Portugal of the Pequenitos, was established. Likewise, under the auspices of the same neighbourhood, one can include the Homestead of Tears *(Quinta das Lágrimas)*, a locale of romantic tastes, which was previously mentioned.

*A conventual church
(18th-century).*

The church of the Santo António dos Olivais
(Igreja de Santo António dos Olivais) (18th-century).

Coimbra is, in fact, also its old suburbs, which, today, are almost all totally integrated into the urban areas and towards which the actual University tends to expand: the University Hospital is to be found in the Celas area, and the Pólo II occupies fields to the south, close by the Mondego. Outside the city were situated convents such as the one from Celas, of medieval origin and which preserves a magnificent cloister. The Franciscan and seventh-century Convent of Santo António dos Olivais is one such convent. Desolate locales, belvederes overlooking valleys, places propitious to reverie, such as the previously mentioned *Penedo da Saudade* or the *Penedo da Meditação*, the latter being squeezed, nowadays, in the row of houses, or even, the *Lapa dos Esteios*, buccolically set out by the river-edge. Buccolic, too, are the *Choupal* and the valley of Canas, fields of pleasure and leisure that the Memmorialist literature of Coimbra does not fail to evoke.

The Santo António dos Olivais Church (Igreja de Santo António dos Olivais) (18th-century). A Franciscan monk.

The fair of Espírito Santo (Feira do Espírito Santo). Ceramics.

The coat of arms of Coimbra.

COIMBRA: A VOYAGE THROUGH HISTORY

The place of implantation of the city of Coimbra may be considered a privileged place from a geographical point of view. A hill and a river are the two elements which served as foundation for the choice of the place on which, and by an ignored people, was founded a village that is at the base of the current city. It comes to pass that the hill on which Coimbra rises, is pratically the one which ends in a continuous line of mountainous ranges which, boasts, among others, of the range of mountains of the Estrela, of Açor, of Lousã, as well as lesser elevations, like the one on which, by the Mondego River, rests the Penacova village. From this hill, downstream, begin the so-called Fields of Mondego *(Campos do Mondego),* low-lying areas which are easily innundated, the majority being marshy, so that in olden times communication in the estuary was made, aboveall, via the fluvial navegation. Besides, Coimbra is, in fact, situated in a zone that is privileged in its contact between the North and the South of the territory, in a narrow zone, and being squeezed between the floodable plain and the range of mountains, on the one hand. On the other hand, Coimbra benefits from its situation as a fluvial port, which serves as intermediary between the villages situated downstream (and the actual sea) and the mountainous interior, which stretches out upstream.
It is not strange to find out, then, that the place from on which the city rose, had been occupied from very early on, even though, truthfully, what previously preceded the Roman *Aeminium/Eminium* is pratically unknown. From the actual *Eminium,* locally, very rare traces are found, which, while still being important, as was the case with the gallery structure which served as support to the forum square ("forum") of the city, the cryptoportico discovered in the Thirties in the inferior part of the old Bishop's Palace *(Paço Episcopal),* the current day Machado de Castro Museum.

A view of Coimbra.

Situated in this crossroads of paths, in the road that linked *Olisipo*/Lisbon to *Braccara Augusta*/Braga, and probably of lesser importance than the neighbourly Conímbriga, Emnium will, thanks to its situation, become the medieval heiress of the latter. In the sixth-century, both the headquarters of the diocese, and the actual name of the city, which, later disappears, transit to *Eminium. Eminium* will come to be designated as Colímbria and, later, as Coimbra.

Already since the beginning of the eighteenth-century, Coimbra, just like the remaining national territory, begins to enjoy the Arabic administration, on the supposition, however, that it will preserve a majority of the population of the Christian faith. Nevertheless, the superiority of the Muslim civilization over the phlegmatic-Roman civilization will lead its inhabitants, although faithful to their professed religion, to adopt the way of living of the newcomers. Coimbra will thus have had a predominantly Muslim Mozarabic population. Conquered definitely, in 1064, by the Christians of the North, the city, being the headquarters of the county, begins to be administered, just like the whole of the septentrional territory, delimited by the Douro river, by Sesnando Davides, a noble Mozarab who had had a notable role in the Muslim court of Seville. Much later, in the twelfth-century, Afonso Henriques, was to make it the capital of the Portuguese kingdom. Headquarters of the University for some time at the beginning of the fourteenth-century, Coimbra becomes its definitive headquarters in 1537, by the decision of King D. João III. This sole fact will endow it with a personality very much of its own, since it was to monopolize the University level of teaching in Portugal for more than three centuries, a monopoly which, pratically, would only be removed after the implementation of the Republic, in 1910.

Conímbriga. The edifice of the Monographic Museum (Museu Monográfico).

CONÍMBRIGA

Conímbriga is one of the Roman cities that have been more widely studied in Portugal. Situated on the *Olisipo-Braccara Augusta* road, the village is dated prior to the Roman presence and was built at the top of a shoulder, bordered by two deep streams of water. Just like the other Lusitanian cities of the Empire, Conímbriga lives in peace for a long time. It benefits from great public works – great edifices that surround the forum *("forum"),* thermal buildings – during the epoch governed by the Ceasar Octavian empire, the Emperor Augustus (30 B.C.-14 A.C.) With the passing of just a couple of decades, the city finds itself ennobled, by means of the construction of a new central public square, a new forum, and by a new set of bathing structures, in the transition from the second-century to the third-century. With the disintegration of the Roman Empire, despite the effort brought to pass by the construction of a strong order of new enclosure walls, Conímbriga is to be invaded and is to be victimised by destruction. In the second half of the fifth-century, the Suevs ransack it and, afterwards, the Visigoths, assault and plunder it. The end of Conímbriga rapidly comes closer. *Eminium (Emínio)* will take its place. It will become the headquarters of the Diocese. Even the actual name of Conímbriga will be usurped. *Eminium* will proceed on its way in History. It will then come to be designated as Coimbra.

Conímbriga. A tank in the museum area.

The House of Fountains (Casa dos Repuxos), with modern coverings, and in a reconstitution of the museum.

Conímbriga. Extra-mural residences.

◄ *An inter-walled residence.*

Alcabideque. The nascent that supplied Conímbriga.